Henry Cornelius Agrippa And His

Exposition Of The Cabala

Henry Morley

Kessinger Publishing's Rare Reprints

Thousands of Scarce and Hard-to-Find Books on These and other Subjects!

- Americana
- Ancient Mysteries
- Animals
- Anthropology
- Architecture
- Arts
- Astrology
- Bibliographies
- Biographies & Memoirs
- Body, Mind & Spirit
- Business & Investing
- Children & Young Adult
- Collectibles
- Comparative Religions
- Crafts & Hobbies
- Earth Sciences
- Education
- Ephemera
- Fiction
- Folklore
- Geography
- Health & Diet
- History
- Hobbies & Leisure
- Humor
- Illustrated Books
- Language & Culture
- Law
- Life Sciences
- Literature
- Medicine & Pharmacy
- Metaphysical
- Music
- Mystery & Crime
- Mythology
- Natural History
- Outdoor & Nature
- Philosophy
- Poetry
- Political Science
- Science
- Psychiatry & Psychology
- Reference
- Religion & Spiritualism
- Rhetoric
- Sacred Books
- Science Fiction
- Science & Technology
- Self-Help
- Social Sciences
- Symbolism
- Theatre & Drama
- Theology
- Travel & Explorations
- War & Military
- Women
- Yoga
- *Plus Much More!*

**We kindly invite you to view our catalog list at:
http://www.kessinger.net**

EXPOSITION OF THE CABALA.

Mainly upon what was said and written by Cornelius Agrippa in this twenty-third year of his age has been founded the defamation by which, when he lived, his spirit was tormented and the hope of his existence miserably frustrated—by which, now that he is dead, his character comes down to us defiled. This victim, at least, has not escaped the vengeance of the monks, and his crime was that he studied vigorously in his salad days those curiosities of learning into which, at the same time, popes, bishops, and philosophers, mature of years, inquired with equal faith and almost equal relish, but less energy or courage. For a clear understanding of the ground, and of the perils of the ground, now taken by Cornelius Agrippa, little more is necessary than a clear notion of what was signified by Reuchlin's book on the Mirific Word; but what has to be said of Reuchlin and his book, as well as of other matters that will hereafter concern the fortunes of Cornelius, requires some previous attention to a subject pretty well forgotten in these days by a people rich in other knowledge; we must recall, in fact, some of the main points of the Cabala.

This account of the Cabala is derived from German sources, among which the chief are Brucker's *Historia Philosophiæ* and the *Kabbala Denudata*, a collection of old cabalistical writings arranged and explained by Christian Knorr von Rosenroth. The traditions, or Cabala, of the Jews, are contained in sundry books, written by Hebrew Rabbis, and consist of a strange mixture of fable and philosophy varying on a good many points, but all adhering with sufficient accuracy to one scheme of doctrine. They claim high and re-mote origin. Some say that the first Cabala were received by Adam from the angel Raziel, who gave him, either while he yet remained in Paradise, or else at the time of his expulsion, to console and help him, a book full of divine wisdom. In this book were the secrets of Nature, and by knowledge of them Adam entered into conversation with the Sun and Moon, knew how to summon good and evil spirits, to inter-pret dreams, foretell events, to heal, and to destroy. This book, handed down from father to son, came into Solomon's possession, and by its aid Solomon became master of many potent secrets. A cabalistic volume, called the Book of Raziel, was, in the middle ages, sometimes to be seen among the Jews.

Another account said that the first cabalistical book was the Sepher Jezirah, written by Abraham; but the most prevalent opinion was, that when the written law was given on Mount Sinai to Moses, the Cabala, or mysterious interpretation of it, was taught to him also. Then Moses, it was said, when he descended from the mountain, entered Aaron's tent, and taught him also the secret powers of the written word; and Aaron, having been instructed, placed himself at the right hand of Moses, and stood by while his sons,

Eleazar and Ithamar, who had been called into the tent, received the same instruction. On the right and left of Moses and Aaron then sat Ithamar and Eleazar, when the seventy elders of the Sanhedrim were called in and taught the hidden knowledge. The elders finally were seated, that they might be present when all those among the common people who desired to learn came to be told those mysteries; thus the elect of the common people heard but once what the Sanhedrim heard twice, the sons of Aaron three times, and Aaron four times repeated of the secrets that had been made known to Moses by the voice of the Most High.

Of this mystical interpretation of the Scripture no person set down any account in writing, unless it was Esdras; but some Jews doubt whether he did. Israelites kept the knowledge of the doctrine by a pure tradition; but about fifty years after the destruction of Jerusalem, Akiba, a great rabbi, wrote the chief part of it in that book, Sepher-jezireh, or the Book of the Creation, which was foolishly ascribed by a few to Abraham. A disciple of the Rabbi Akiba was Rabbi Simeon ben Jochai, who wrote more of the tradition in a book called Zoar.

The truth probably is, that the literature of cabalism, which is full of suggestion derived from the Neoplatonics of Alexandria, began with the Jews of Alexandria under the first Ptolemys. In the book of Simeon ben Schetach it went to Palestine, where it at first was little heeded; but after the destruction of Jerusalem it gained importance, and then Rabbis Akiba and Simeon ben Jochai extended it. It is indisputable that Aristotle had been studied by the writer of the Sepher-jezireh, the oldest known book of the Cabalists. The Cabala went afterwards with other learning to Spain, and that part of it at least which deals wu h Hebrew anagrams cannot be traced to a time earlier than the eleventh century. Many rabbis —Abraham ben David, Saudia, Moses Botril, Moses bar Nachman, Eliezer of Garmiza, and others—have written Hebrew books for the purpose of interpreting the system of the Cabala; but it was, perhaps, not before the eighth century that it had come to receive very general attention from the Jews.

The Cabala consisted of two portions, the symbolical and the real; the symbolical Cabala being the means by which the doctrines of the real Cabala were elicited.

In the Hebrew text of the Scriptures, it was said, there is not only an evident, but there is also a latent meaning; and in its latent meaning are contained the mysteries of God and of the universe. It need scarcely be said that a belief in secret wisdom has for ages been inherent in the Oriental mind, and in the Scriptures, it was reasoned by the the later Jews, all wisdom must be, of necessity, contained. Of divine authorship, they cannot be like ordinary works of men. But if they were taken only in the natural sense, might it not be said that many human works contain marvels not less surprising and morality as pure. No, it was said, as we have entertained angels, and regarded them as men, so we may entertain the words of the Most High, if we regard only their apparent sense and not their spiritual mystery. And so it was that through a blind excess of reverence the inspired writings were put to superstitious use.

The modes of examining their letters, words, and sentences, for hidden meaning, in which wholly consisted the symbolical Cabala, were three, and these were called Gemantria, Notaricon, Themura

Gemantria was arithmetical when it consisted in applying to the Hebrew letters of a word the sense they bore as numbers, letters being used also for figures in the Hebrew as in the Greek. Then the letters in a word being taken as numbers and added up, it was considered that another word, of which the letters added up came to an equal sum, might fairly be substituted by the arithmetical gemantria. Figurative gemantria deduced mysterious interpretations from the shapes of letters used in sacred writing. Thus, in Numbers x., 35, Beth means the reversal of enemies. This kind of interpretation was known also by the name of Zurah. Architectonic gemantria constructed words from the numbers given by Scripture when describing the measurements of buildings, as the ark, or temple.

By Notaricon more words were developed from the letters of a word, as if it had consisted of so many abbreviations, or else first and last letters of words, or the first letters of successive words, were detached from their places and put side by side. By Themura, any word might be made to yield a mystery out of its anagram; these sacred anagrams were known as Zeruph. By the same branch of the symbolical Cabala three systems were furnished, in accordance with which words might be transformed by the substitution of one letter for another. The first of the systems, Albam, arranged the letters of the alphabet in two rows, one below another; the second, Athbath, gave another couple of rows; the third, Athbach, arranged them by pairs in three rows—all the pairs in the first row being the numerical value ten, in the second row a hundred, in the third a thousand; any one of these forms might be consulted, and any letter in a word exchanged for another standing either in Albam, Athbath, or Athbach, immediately above it or below it, or on the right hand of it or the left.

This was the symbolical Cabala, and the business of

16

it was to extract, by any of the means allowed, the hidden meaning of the Scriptures. The real Cabala was the doctrine in this way elicited. It was theoretical, explaining divine qualities, the ten sephiroth, the fourfold cabalistical worlds, the thirty-two footprints of wisdom, the fifty doors to prudence, Adam Kadmon, &c. ; or it was practical, explaining how to use such knowledge for the calling of spirits, the extinguishing of fires, the banishing of disease, and so forth.

The theoretical Cabala contained, it was said by Christian students, many references to the Messiah. Its main points were: 1—The Tree; 2—The Chariot of Ezekiel; 3—The Work of Creation; 4—The Ancient of Days mentioned in Daniel. It concerns us most to understand the Tree. The Chariot of Ezekiel, or Maasseh Mercabáh, was a description of prefigurements concerning ceremonial and judicial law. The doctrine of Creation, in the book Levischith, was a dissertation upon physics. The Ancient of Days treated of God and the Messiah in a way so mystical that cabalists generally declined to ascribe any meaning at all to the direct sense of the words employed. Of these things we need say no more, but of the Cabalistical Tree it will be requisite to speak in more detail.

It was an arrangement of the ten sephiroth. The word Sephiroth is derived by some rabbis from a word meaning to count, because they are a counting of the divine excellence. Otherwise it is considered an adaptation of the Greek word Sphere, because it represents the spheres of the universe which are successive emanations from the Deity.

In the beginning was Or Haensoph, the eternal light, from whose brightness there descended a ray through the first-born of God, Adam Kadmon, and presently, departing from its straight course, ran in a circle, and so formed the first of the sephiroth, which was called

Kethei, or the crown, because superior to all the rest. Having formed this circle, the ray resumed its straight course till it again ran in a circle to produce the second of the ten sephiroth, Chochma, wisdom, because wisdom is the source of all. The same ray of divine light passed on, losing gradually, as it became more distant from its holy source, some of its power, and formed presently, in like manner, the third of the sephiroth, called Binah, or understanding, because understanding is the channel through which wisdom flows to things below—the origin of human knowledge. The fourth of the sephiroth is called Gedolah or Chesed, greatness or goodness, because God, as being great and good, created all things. The fifth is Geburah, strength, because it is by strength that He maintains them, and because strength is the only source of justice in the world. The sixth of the sephiroth, Thpereth, beauty or grace, unites the qualities of the preceding. The four last of the sephiroth are successively named Nezach, victory; Hod, honor; Jesod, or Schalom, the foundation or peace; and finally, Malcuth, the kingdom. Each of the ten has also a divine name, and their divine names, written in the same order, are Ejeh, Jah, Jehovah (pronounced Elohim), Eloah, Elohim, Jehovah (pronounced as usual), Lord Sabaoth, Jehovah Zebaoth, Elchai (the living God), Adonai (the Lord). By these circles our world is surrounded, and, weakened in its passage through them, but able to bring down with it powers that are the character of each, divine light reaches us. These sephiroth, arranged in a peculiar manner, form the Tree of the Cabalists; they are also sometimes arranged in the form of a man, Adam Kadmon, according to the idea of the Neoplatonics that the figure of the world was that of a man's body. In accordance with another view derived from the same school, things in this world were supposed to be gross images of things above. Matter was said by the cabalists to have been formed by the withdrawal of the divine ray, by the emanation of which from the first source it was produced. Everything created was created by an emanation from the source of all, and that which being most distant contains least of the divine essence is capable of gradual purification; so that even the evil spirits will in course of time become holy and pure, and be assimilated to the brightest of the emanations from Or Haensoph. God, it was said, is all in all; everything is part of the divine essence, with a growing, or perceptive, or reflective power, one or all, and by that which has one all may be acquired. A stone may become a plant; a plant, a beast; a beast, a man; a man, an angel; an angel, a creator.

This kind of belief, which was derived also from the Alexandrian Platonists led to that spiritual cabalism by which such Christians as Reuchlin and Agrippa profited. It connected them by a strong link with the divine essence, and they, feeling perhaps more distinctly than their neighbors that they were partakers of the divine nature, and might, by a striving after purity of soul and body win their way to a state of spiritual happiness and power, cut themselves off from all communion with the sensuality that had become the scandal of the Church of Rome, and keenly perceived, as they expressed strongly, their sense of the degraded habits of the priests. It was in this way that the Christian Cabalists assisted in the labors of the Reformation.

Little more has to be said about their theory, and that relates to the four Cabalistical Worlds. These were placed in the four spaces between the upper sephiroth. Between the first and second was placed Aziluth, the outflowing, which contained the purest

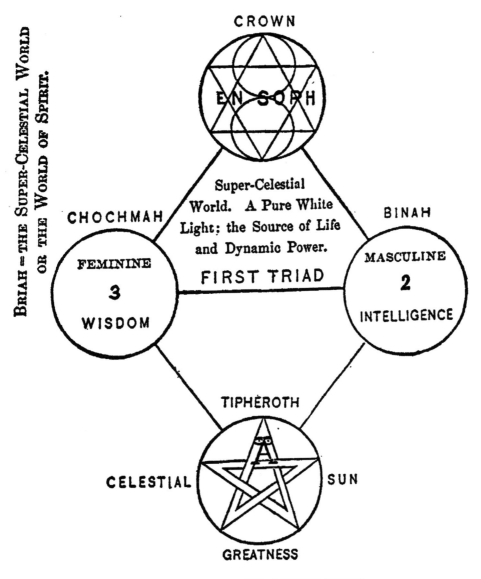

FIRST TO FOURTH SEPHIROTH.

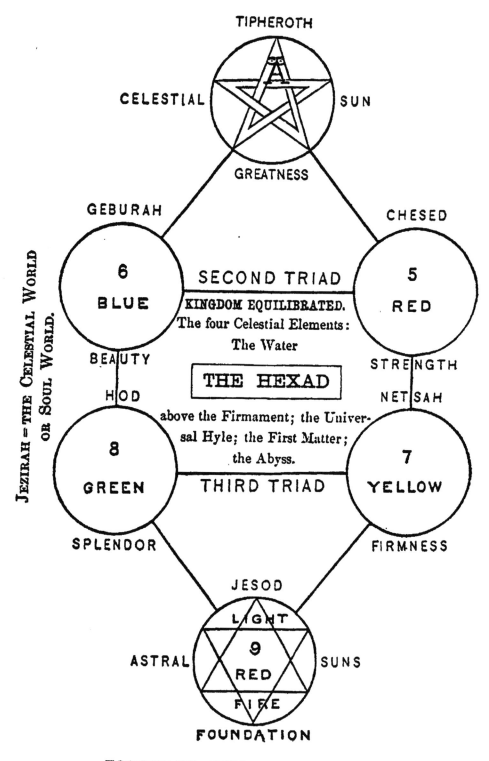

FOURTH TO NINTH SEPHIROTH.

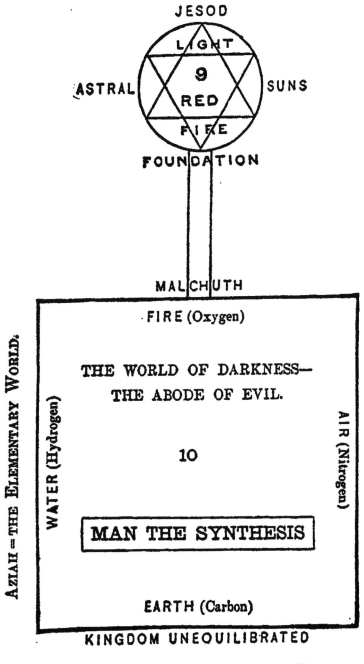

NINTH AND TENTH SEPHIROTH.

beings, the producers of the rest. Between the second and third sephiroth was the world Briah, or the thrones, containing spirits less pure, but still not material. They were classed into wheels, lightnings, lions, burning spirits, angels, children of God, cherubim. Their prince was called Metatron. The world in the next interspace, called Jezireh, angels, approached more nearly to a material form; and the fourth, Asiah, was made wholly material. From this point density increases till our world is reached. Asiah is the abode of the Klippoth, or material spirits striving against God. They travel through the air, their bodies are of dense air, incorruptible, and they have power to work in the material world. With Catoriel, Adam Belial, Esau, Aganiel, Usiel, Ogiel, Thomiel, Theumiel, for captains, they fight in two armies under their chiefs Zamiel and Lilith. Their enemies are the angels, who contend against them with two armies, led by Metatron and Sandalphon. Lilith is the begetter of the powers striving against light.

The nature of man's soul, said Cabalists, is three-fold—vegetative, perceptive, intellectual—each embracing each. It emanates from the upper sephiroth, is composed of the pure elements—for the four elements, either in their pure and spiritual or their gross form, enter into all things—is expansive, separates after death, so that the parts return each to its own place, but reunite to praise God on the sabbaths and new moons. With each soul are sent into the world a guardian and an accusing angel.

NOTE: Mr. Morley's excellent summary of the Kabbala Denudata may be regarded as fully authentic although he writes from the standpoint of an unbeliever. The Tree of the Cabala (divided into three plates to facilitate comparison), by Dr. Pancoast, gives the more modern rendition of the Cabala. We introduce, on the two following pages, a newly arranged table of the Cabala (Hebrew letters) renderings in English letters, symbols, tarot emblems, etc. This table is the plainest in its terms of all others. Following the table the Cabala is continued under the title of "The Mirific Word."

A NEWLY ARRANGED TABLE

NUMERICAL ORDER.	HEBREW FORM.	LETTERS. NAME.	CORRESPONDING ENGLISH.	NUMERICAL VALUE.
1	א	Aleph	A	1
2	ב	Beth	B, BH, BY	2
3	ג	Gimel	G, GH	3
4	ד	Daleth	D, DH	4
5	ה	He	H	5
6	ו	Vau	V, W	6
7	ז	Zayin	Z	7
8	ח	Cheth	CH, KH, HH, H	8
9	ט	Teth	T	9
10	י	Yodh	Y, I, J	1C
11	כ	Caph	C, CH, K, KH	20
12	ל	Lamed	L	30
13	מ	Mem	M	40
14	נ	Nun	N	50
15	ס	Samech	S	60
16	ע	Ayin	O, GHH	70
17	פ	Phe	P, PH	80
18	צ	Tsadhe	TS, TZ	90
19	ק	Koph	K, Q	100
20	ר	Resh	R, RH	200
0	ש	Shin	S, SH	300
21	ת	Tau	T, TH	400

☞ Five Hebrew Letters, Caph, Mem, Nun, Phe, and

OF THE TAROT AND CABALA.

SYMBOLS.	TAROT MEANINGS.	CLASSES.
Bull	The Magician	Mother
House	High Priestess	Double
Erect Serpent	The Empress	Double
Door or Hinge	The Emperor	Double
Window, Virginity	The Hierophant	Single
Nail, Hook	The Lovers	Single
Weapon	The War Chariot	Single
Fence	Justice	Single
Scrotum	The Hermit	Single
Male Organs	Wheel of Fate	Single
Hollow of Hand, Cube	Strength	Double
Ox-goad, Whip	The Suspended Man	Single
Water	Death	Mother
Fish	Temperance	Single
Pillar, Egg	The Demon	Single
Eye	Lightning-struck tower	Single
Mouth	The Star	Double
Fish-hook, Dart	The Moon	Single
Back Scull	The Sun	Single
Head, Sphere, Circle	Judgment	Double
Tooth	The Zany	Mother
Cross	The Universe	Double

Tsadhe, denote 500, 600, 700, 800, and 900, when final.

CPSIA information can be obtained
at www.ICGtesting.com
Printed in the USA
391071LV00001B/4

9 781430 414285